D1084543

THE ALCHEMY OF WOMAN HOOD

DOLORES RICE

COVER ART BY SU BLACKWELL

THE ALCHEMY

1: POWER TO TRANSFORM SOMETHING
COMMON INTO SOMETHING SPECIAL

2: medieval science and philosophy aiming to achieve the transmutation
of base metals into gold, the discovery of a universal cure for disease,
and the discovery of a means of indefinitely prolonging life.

OF WOMAN

1. *A female human being*

HOOD

1: A collective or community of which something is part
2: A state that one finds one's self in

FOR WILLOW

. . . and daughters everywhere

Listen, child, listen to what I have to tell you, for a child you will soon be no more.

So soon you will become a woman and the part of you that listens well to me now will begin to listen to other voices, voices that become loud in your environment, voices that you choose to hear, voices that speak to you in other ways than I. So listen to me now, before that time comes, for what I will tell you in these pages is sacred, a gift to you, that you have a right to, that I merely pass on as your mother, a mother like all mothers who wants all that is good for you, who hopes to give you wisdom that will serve you as you grow and become a woman yourself ♡

I want you to know this knowledge now so you can bury it deep inside of you ⊠ *So you will have the answers you need when you need them* ◻ THIS KNOWEDGE COMES FROM ALL WOMEN WHO HAVE BEEN AND KNOWN AND HAVE PASSED IT ON TO ME. ALL OF THIS KNOWL-EDGE I HAVE VERIFIED AND KNOW TO BE TRUE. I WOULD NOT TELL YOU AN UNTRUTH AT THIS STAGE OF YOUR BECOMING. ONLY THE RIGOR OF WHAT I KNOW TO BE TRUE IS WORTHY OF YOUR LISTENING. *So I endeavor to offer you that.*

Since you were a baby, I have discovered that for every moment in your life that you become more of who you are, I have to let you go a little more.

YOU WERE INSIDE OF ME, THEN OUTSIDE OF ME, IN MY BED, THEN IN YOUR OWN, IN OUR HOUSE THEN IN YOUR SCHOOL, TELLING ME EVERYTHING, THEN TELLING YOUR FRIENDS, AND ALL OF THIS IS THE WAY IT SHOULD BE.

I am here to encourage you to grow and fully become your own being. I hand you over this knowledge so as you may become a woman who can move freely with confidence and fluidity, a woman who may eventually hold her own child's hand crossing the street and no longer need mine to hold, a woman who is joyfully in charge of her own life and of her own body.

AS A MOTHER, BY
LETTING GO, I AM
TEACHING YOU ALSO
TO LET GO.

BUT BEFORE THIS LETTING-GO, I WOULD
LIKE TO ENSURE THAT I HAVE FIRST
ENDOWED YOU WITH THE TOOLS YOU
WILL NEED TO WALK THIS WORLD WITH
GRACE AND STRENGTH.

YES, DAUGHTER, THIS IS MY GIFT TO YOU.
The gift of knowledge, a sweet form of knowledge
that I am passing on while you are still open to me,
as a daughter is to a mother before she becomes a
woman herself and begins to discover the world in
her own unique way, listening to the rhythms of your
heart and listening to those that seem to dance to
the same beat as you. And sometimes mothers don't
seem to do that, but that's alright. When the time
comes for you to strike up on your own and away
from me, I will remain here, in your background,
going about my day, while keeping a place of stillness, ready to hold you if ever you need it and always
on your side as you travel through life in all its magic
and all its adventures.

While you still lie in my arms at night drifting off to sleep let me tell you a bit of what I have discovered about being female in this world, first a girl, then a woman, then a mother. Your mother.

AND WHAT A GIFT YOU ARE TO ME ▧

WOMEN HAVE
A POWER
THAT DOES
NOT NEED
TO TURN
TO VIOLENCE
TO MAKE
AN IMPACT.

In the hidden drawer of your being there is a fold, like a fold in time. I want to take you through it now, as I have been to the other side. I want to guide your passage with wisdom. I want to layer you with a knowledge that, though just beyond your reach, will remain inside of you for some point in the future and if you doubt what you remember, you will have this book as a place to come back to *A safe place, full of the wisdom to which women have been returning since time began. A sacred place of beauty and truth and above all power.*

WOMEN KNOW THE ESSENCE OF CREATION.

Women know that to be the best of themselves they need only stop, listen deeply, find within themselves the seed of some creation bursting to come forth, and honor it, in order to become a valuable addition to the world.

Women's bodies are in a constant state of churning what will inevitably be the evolution of the human race. It is each woman's choice whether their contribution to that evolution is a graceful one or not. For everything we do, say, create, is a contribution to the world. And what beauty there is in contributing mindfully, wholly, with reverence for those around us. What other purpose is there than to have left the world a better place after it is time for us to go?

There have been countless religions and ideologies, cultures and peoples that have tried to describe women in ways that are less than powerful; these are merely fearful reactions to women's strength.

Some times and places and peoples have tried to treat a woman's body as less than sacred, less than the sole giver of life. They have failed to see that a woman's body is in essence sacred, is in essence power, is in essence at the centre of the lifeforce. All that is could not be without woman in all her churning forces of being ▣

THIS IS ALWAYS AND
FOREVER MORE SO.
THIS IS OUR NATURE
AS WOMEN. THIS IS
OUR BIRTHRIGHT.
THIS IS WHAT BEING
A FEMALE HUMAN
AMOUNTS TO IN ALL
ITS GLORY.

WOMAN

I.
A FEMALE
HUMAN
BEING

womb

vulva

bleed

waves

moon

body

beginning

womb

There is a womb inside of you. This womb is what makes you a woman. There is a beauty in this place, a sacred, holy beauty to which you have access now and always. This most sacred chamber is nestled between your hip bones, sitting atop your vagina. Inside of it, life is created and grows.

THIS WOMB IS AN EVERCHANGING CHAMBER
FULL OF ACTIVITY AND MOVEMENT, RICH AND
MAGICAL AND ALIVE ⬚ *It holds the key to your well-being and is the intelligence of your soul* ✳ Its very fabric
sings with intuition for you to absorb, an inner voice speaking
to you its wisdom, a wisdom that may sound very different
to all the logical voices clamoring for attention on the outside,
a wisdom that is your unique key to unlock what is truth for
you and often true for the world.

THERE IS A LAB INSIDE
OF THIS WOMB, WHERE
A SACRED APPARATUS
MADE UP OF TUBES AND
ANTECHAMBERS EXISTS,
WHERE THE FINEST OF
EXPERIMENTS TAKES
PLACE AND WHERE YOU
YIELD PURE GOLD.

INSIDE OF YOU RESIDES
THE VERY ELIXIR OF LIFE.

WITHIN YOUR BODY,
ALCHEMY IS AT WORK.

Men contribute an equal, an essential and a significant part of the alchemy ✳ *But inside of you is different from inside your male friends, in the way your body is shaped and in the work it does* ⊞ You are formed to be able to receive what a man has to offer and then to take their offering and turn it into life. You have been endowed by nature with this womb, this central chamber of our species' alchemy, this chamber within which, without much ado, you transform basic matter into gold.

FOR WOMEN ARE THE ALCHEMISTS·THEY HAVE LONG AGO KNOWN THE PHILOSOPHER'S STONE· THEY CARRY WITHIN THEM THE SECRET TO LIFE · THEIR BODIES ARE THE VERY BEGINNING, MIDDLE AND END OF EXISTENCE · TOGETHER THEY ARE WHAT MAKES THE WORLD TURN · THEY CONNECT IN THE MOST PROFOUND WAY WITH ALL THAT IS POWER ON THIS PLANET AND CAN, WITHOUT GREAT EFFORT, GENERATE ALL THAT IS LIFE ·

vulva

The external gateway to this womb are the lips of your vulva. Your vulva is one of the most private parts of your anatomy because it is the gateway to your womb.

It is quite probable that you have already begun exploring your vulva, its lips called the labia, a small protruding tip called the clitoris, the entire protruding part of your vagina, that makes up the soft flesh between your legs. And you have probably already noticed that when you touch this area of your body, you may be filled with a powerful, tingling sensation of warmth and generosity. *This sensation will never go away.* THIS IS YOURS FOREVER AND ALWAYS AND BELONGS TO YOU ▣

NO ONE ELSE CAN GIVE THIS TO YOU
OR TAKE IT AWAY.

WHEN YOU BECOME A MATURE WOMAN, YOU
LEARN TO SHARE THIS AND OTHER SENSATIONS
WITH ANOTHER. BUT ONLY IF AND WHEN YOU
GIVE ANOTHER PERMISSION ▣ It is through this
kind of sharing that men and women make the connections
which allow a woman to receive from a man that which she
needs to create another life. But that is a long way off for
now. For now, what is important to know is that your vulva
is your very personal and private gateway to your womb.
▣ *And every girl's and then woman's is shaped differently,
reflecting who they are perfectly.*

Your vulva opens up and leads into a passageway called the vagina. Toward the end of this passageway, there is an inner gate named the cervix which is the potent final entrance to the womb. Once inside this womb there are other gateways, other passageways there to allow the comings and goings of all that goes into the alchemy of a woman's body. Let me tell you something of those.

When baby girls arrive into the world, they carry inside of them millions of tiny, golden eggs in two holding pods called the ovaries. The baby girl grows and grows into a young girl, then grows and grows into a young woman until one day, she enters a phase in her growth called Menarche: the onset of menstruation, when her body decides that the time is right to start releasing some of these golden eggs, marking the start of an adventure which, for the first several years, will end not in the creation of new life, but rather in the habituation of the body to the process of menstruation.

The eggs' holding pods are called ovaries. They sit to the right and sit to the left of the womb like two princesses on each side of their queen. These ovaries, filled with the golden eggs named ovums, are linked to the womb through tubes. These tubes allow these ovums to travel along their special corridors into the womb. These tubes are called fallopian tubes.

Through these very special fallopian pathways, the golden eggs make their journey from the ovary to the womb.

bleed

These golden eggs that will soon be released in your body, when you experience your first menstrual cycle, when you get what we call your "period" for the first time, will begin by creating pathways for future adventures, laying the foundations for a fertile ground, making your womb rich with nutrients and keeping the sacred vessel of your body alive and nourished so when you are eventually mature and ready, you can enjoy it in the fullest possible way.

Menstruation is the process by which every month, your body, all on its own, will release some of these golden eggs, every month of every year until when you're much older, you may become pregnant and the eggs take a pause while the baby is growing inside and then outside for a while, or indeed later again in your journey as a woman when all the eggs are gone and menstruation stops as you move into another phase of womanhood called menopause.

But let us return to the phase you will enter into soon. Menarche.

Every month at the beginning of any woman's menstrual cycle, her womb lines itself with an extrasoft layer of red matter in preparation for the arrival of a golden egg from her ovaries. Once this cushion is in place, the golden egg is released in a process called ovulation, knowing that if it fuses with a male sperm and needs somewhere to rest and grow, the inner landscape of her womb is ready to hold it.

BUT FOR A YOUNG WOMEN SUCH AS YOU WHO IS JUST STARTING OUT ON THIS ADVENTURE, the egg is released and continues on its journey down through the fallopian path into the sacred chamber, encountering no male sperm with which to connect; and therefore, no need to stop and rest in the soft cushion the womb has created ⊠ *As your egg does not need this cocoon in which to develop and grow, it continues onward signaling to these layers that they are not needed at this time* ⊠ Upon receiving this signal, the layers release from the walls of the womb, trailing the egg as though the egg were a child who had gathered its safety blanket and dragged it along the hallway.

The egg and the liquid layer flow out of your body in the form of a rich, dark-red blood for several days until the chamber is cleared of the generous layer that is unnecessary this cycle, cleansing itself in preparation for the next cycle, over and over again, each month until a time comes when well into mature womanhood, an egg may meet a male sperm and the layered cushion, so rich at this stage from its constant motion of building and letting go, like a vibrant forest floor, can hold a joined egg and sperm in its cradle for over nine months while a human life is formed inside of the woman's womb, her belly expanding to make room for the baby within.

There are many ways a male sperm can meet this egg but one of the most common is through a physical connection between man and woman. In time, when the male sexual organ, the penis, enters through the vulva, into the vagina penetrating the cervix carrying with it a male sperm, which it may release, one of those sperms may meet one of these golden eggs inside this sacred space of the womb and fuse together to create what may someday, become another human being, like a prince being presented at court before the queen, offering his hand in marriage to one of the princesses.

BUT THIS COURTLY PRESENTATION IS A LONG
WAY OFF FOR YOU MY DAUGHTER.

I MENTION IT NOW ONLY SO YOU MAY POSSESS
THE KNOWLEDGE IN ITS TRUTH.

LIKE EVERYTHING
IN OUR NATURAL
WORLD, THERE IS
A RHYTHM OF
EXPANSION AND
CONTRACTION,
GETTING BIGGER
AND GETTING
SMALLER,
BREATHING OUT,
BREATHING IN.

A WOMAN'S BODY IS NO DIFFERENT.

A woman's body is like the moon, and the ocean, part of a profound cycle which allows it to yield enormous treasures, gathering and letting go.

WHEN WE PAY ATTENTION
TO EACH PART OF THEIR
JOURNEY, THESE GOLDEN
EGGS WILL GUIDE US LIKE
WISE TEACHERS ON HOW
TO BE IN THE WORLD.

waves

Your body's cycle can serve as your guide on how to be in both your inner and outer life. For female bodies cycle through four very different waves during this menstrual cycle: one of preparation, one of action, one of retreat and one of rest.

Listen and behold how you are in each phase.

IN THE FIRST WAVE OF PREPARATION, it may be that while your body is preparing, gathering the matter to make up the cushion that will soften the egg's journey, that you too will find it easier to begin and plan your activities in the world.

IN THE SECOND WAVE OF ACTION, when your body is springing into ovulation, releasing the golden egg knowing that it has prepared well for its arrival, that you too will be at your strongest out in the world, offering up your well-thought-out plans.

THEN, WHEN YOUR BODY WANTS TO BEGIN ITS INNER RETREAT, as the egg finds no sperm to marry, readying itself for the letting go of its layer, perhaps you too will want to let go and conclude plans, projects, thoughts, ideas and quieten inside to get ready for the next wave.

IN THE FINAL WAVE OF REST, when your body releases all its hard work into the past in a deep process of letting go through the bleed, perhaps you too would do best to rest in order to get ready for the next phase of preparation, action, retreat and rest in both your inner and outer life.

These waves will move within you, sometimes causing you to feel unsteady, or sensitive, or as though tears are the only conversation, but know that this is how your body speaks to you, for you, because of you, always on your behalf. Your body's conversation has a truth and a purpose. Trust it to know better ▨

AND SO WE CYCLE ON LIKE ALL BEINGS IN NATURE.

THIS IS THE RHYTHM OF OUR BODY.

THIS IS THE RHYTHM OF WOMAN.

THIS IS THE RHYTHM OF ALCHEMY.[1]

[1] *These waves correspond to the ancient alchemical process.* **THE NIGREDO PHASE,** the darkening through decomposition, is mirrored by the unfertilized egg disengaging itself, thereby informing the cushion to do the same. Then comes **THE RUBEDO PHASE**, the reddening, when the egg and the lining merge together in a river of blood to leave the body; thus leaving the chambers cleared, so the body enters **THE ALBEDO PHASE**, the purification, ready and prepared for the elixir of life, the golden egg, to appear, which brings us to **THE CITRINITAS PHASE.** This is the final golden phase of the alchemical process, the release of the golden egg, the source of life.

For some young women, they will feel most at home in a time of preparation, for some, action will be their strong suit, others thrive in the gentleness of retreat and still others in the stillness of rest ◻ *Whichever feels most home to you, always be aware of the time and revere it for what it is* FOR IT IS YOUR BODY IN ITS FULLEST EXPRESSION AND YOU ARE ITS GREATEST ADVOCATE ◻

At times, the world around you may not be in sync with your rhythm. It may appear that it does not even respect it. What counts is that you discover your pace, acknowledge it, get to know and understand it, taking care of its needs. Listening to your voice and moving with your internal rhythms will allow you to journey through life in the most gentle way possible.

moon

As the moon cycles through her different phases over a 29-day period, so will you cycle through your menstrual phases over a 29 day period. In an era before artificial light, food and rhythms, Women would align with the moon, often menstruating on the new moon, a time of deep rest and reflection, and ovulating on a full moon, a time of expansiveness and radiant light. Find a way to see the moon in your evening time. Observe it and its transforming shapes. Be aware of your stage in your cycle and see how it coincides with the moon's. How does the moon look when you begin your bleed; how does it look when it finishes? When you feel the burst of energy of ovulation, does the moon reflect it in a radiant fullness? Or is it a quieter expression on both your parts? And the time just before you bleed, when the world seems to reveal itself to you in the most heightened of ways, how is the moon then? You will see month after month that she is there for you, your friend throughout menstruation, a knowing light in the sky, a place to which you can turn for stillness and wisdom.

There is an evident power in this.

What other being on the planet has such conscious connection to the power of the moon and shares its rhythms only with the ocean?

Endow yourself with this gift. Connect with the world on this profound level. What a source of strength this could provide as you move through life, growing and dreaming and wanting and being.

THE MOON AWAITS YOU,
SEEK HER OUT.

body

As these internal changes happen to your body, so too do some very beautiful external changes. Your womanly form begins to emerge.

Over the next few years you will notice hair beginning to grow around your pubic area, the area surrounding your vulva. First a light covering and then fuller. This hair is there to protect your precious gateway, to keep it warm and to become part of how your body expresses itself as you get older. At the same time as the hair begins to grow here, hair will begin to grow under your arms.

Many young women choose to eliminate this hair through various forms of hair removal, and some remove some of the pubic hair around the vulva too and many remove the hair on their legs ⬚ *These are all very personal and private choices that should be arrived at after much consideration and never because everyone else is doing it* ⬚ Especially in the case of your pubic area, which is so delicate and sensitive, attuned to your needs.

For millennia women and men around the globe have practiced the art of hair removal, from men shaving their beards to women waxing off their pubic hair and every other hair follicle in-between for both sexes. At some stage every section of the body has in some place or time been stripped of its hair. As a young woman, you will certainly encounter all forms of suggestion as to how you should treat *your* hair

This is not something to take lightly nor to approach without professional advice but please remember at all times that no hair need ever be removed, that all decisions that are possible to make as to how much hair you decide to leave or remove from your body should be yours and yours alone and all of them are perfect ☑

IT IS YOUR BODY AND
IT SHOULD FEEL AS YOU
WANT IT TO FEEL, LOOK
AS YOU WANT IT TO
LOOK, BE AS YOU WANT
IT TO BE.

Indeed, there is a huge business in hair removal, in fashion, in makeup that is designed to take advantage of young people's uncertainty about how they "should" appear. *If there was one thing to say about the advertiser-commentator it is this*: their job is to use your body's innate functionality against you: it is only that which your body must do that can be guaranteed as a tool to turn against you over and over again. Own your innate functionality and know the strength it gives you. Never believe ever that it takes anything away ⬛⬛

ADVERTISEMENTS THAT
ARE DESIGNED TO MAKE
YOU THINK
THAT YOU HAVE:
TOO MUCH HAIR,
TOO LITTLE HAIR,
YOU SMELL TOO MUCH,
SMELL TO LITTLE,
LOOK TOO SMALL,
LOOK TOO BIG;

ALL OF THEM ARE FALSE.

There is not a creative director in a commercial department that does not know how to redirect self-questioning and fear into consumerism. There are so many beautiful things out there, clothes, makeup, jewelry, hair products, skin products, gadgets, etc . . . etc . . . but really listen within yourself when you see you want something ⊞ *Do you want to consume because doing so will be a celebration of you and who you are, or is it because you believe that what you want to consume will, in some way, change who you are?*

NOTHING ON THE OUT-
SIDE WILL CHANGE YOU
ON THE INSIDE AND
THERE IS NO RIGHT WAY
TO APPEAR.

THE MOST BEAUTIFUL
AND POWERFUL WOMEN
IN THE WORLD TODAY
ARE SO BECAUSE THEY
KNOW, IN THE DEEPEST
PLACE ONE CAN KNOW,
THAT THEY ARE BEAU-
TIFUL AND POWERFUL,
JUST LIKE YOU.

THE WORLD AS IT TURNS NOW, SO FILLED WITH IMAGES AND SUPPOSED IDEALS CAN FEEL LIKE A PRECARIOUS PLACE IN WHICH TO BECOME A WOMAN. BUT THE ESSENCE OF WOMANHOOD IS ALWAYS SAFE IN THE ARMS OF SELF-KNOWLEDGE. ALL ALONG THE PATH THERE WILL BE RABBITHOLES OF SELF-DOUBT LURING YOU IN, TRYING TO MAKE YOU FORGET.

It remains hard for us not to be swayed by arguments presented so convincingly and often so beautifully in all forms of media and in life itself. ⚏ BUT WHEN YOU ARE SWAYED, BECAUSE YOU WILL BE, ALWAYS COME BACK TO YOUR QUIET PLACE AND REMIND YOURSELF OF HOW PERFECT YOU ARE NO MATTER HOW YOU AFFECT YOUR BODY ◐ *For now and for always, your body knows exactly what to do for the wellbeing of You* ◐ LEARN TO LISTEN TO IT.

THAT IS THE TRUTH AND WILL ALWAYS BE SO.

Soon your breasts will start burgeoning. Like buds they will start to rise from the flat surface of your chest and continue to do so until they reach the perfect size for your body ▧

Everyone's body is unique and every young woman's breasts are unique, some seeming smaller, rounder, bigger, longer, looser, tighter, thicker, wider, thinner, with nipples that are pointier, flatter, rounder, straighter, some with larger areolae, smaller areolae, no two breasts the same, and yet, every set perfect. Sometimes around the time of your menstrual bleed, they may get more sensitive, more tender. And your breasts will change over time as will the rest of your body, but they will always be perfectly in keeping with who you are.

The form of your body will also become softer and fuller as you get ready to menstruate.

A woman's body needs an extra layer filled with delicious nutrients in order to support the release of healthy eggs. Without this layer, eggs may not release. This layer needs to be there to sustain menstruation month after month. Celebrate your fuller womanly form. It gives you power. It supports the life-force flowing through you.

The more womanly you become, the more changes you will see in what your body releases. Many consistencies of fluids will leave your body from your vagina throughout the month depending what is happening in your womb. Every fluid is the perfect outcome of your body's innate ability to ready itself for your use. Over time, as you observe, you will come to know what each consistency means, you will find changes in smell that are there to communicate to you your body's current state. Again, there will be missives from the world at large to condemn smells, discharges, and all things womanly.

IT IS UP
TO YOU
TO LISTEN
WITH YOUR
OWN DEEP
KNOWLEDGE.

L ISTEN FOR SIGNS OF SELF-INTEREST IN ALL OFFERINGS. IS IT A GIFT FOR YOUR BODY OR IS IT SOMETHING THAT DESIRES TO TAKE SOMETHING FROM YOU, MAKE YOU FEEL LESS THAN? ONLY ACCEPT GIFTS ⧈

Likewise, never do a disservice to another girl or woman by commenting negatively about any of her bodily functions or states. Even if they are unrecognizable to you, or make you feel uncomfortable, her body is as sacred as yours in its difference and deserves your reverence and respect. Once you know this, it is your profound mission to never unknow it, thereby strengthening the ground on which all women walk and coexist.

YOUR BODY IS YOUR BODY. IT SHOULD ALWAYS BE FOR YOU TO DETERMINE HOW TO TREAT IT. IT IS ALWAYS YOUR CHOICE AS TO WHAT SHOULD TOUCH IT. YOUR CHOICE AS TO WHAT ENTERS YOUR VAGINA. AND ALSO YOUR CHOICE AS TO HOW WHAT EXITS, LEAVES.

The first substance that will leave your vagina will be the blood of the menstrual cycle.

This blood starts out as a couple of drops to announce its arrival and then gets heavy and rich. It then thins out becoming increasingly lighter over a four to seven day period and then stops for roughly three weeks, depending on the regularity of your cycle. On day one of your cycle your bleed will start up again with a few drops and so on and so forth.

There are many ways to deal with the bleed as it leaves your body, but the three most common are the tampon, the sanitary napkin and the mooncup.

In ancient Egypt women made tampons from papyrus. In the times in between many other natural fibers have been used for absorbing menstrual flow. This will be a very pragmatic part of your journey, to chose which method feels best for you.

Like with all selfcare, the more naturally treated the materials are that enter and touch your body, the less you upset the balance of your organism.

The more freely the blood can flow out of your body and the less stagnation incurred, the better it is for a woman's emotional fluidity.

Your vagina and your vulva are deeply sensitive. Treat them with the care they deserve when choosing how to absorb your bleed.

Tampons, for the most part, come in the form of a cotton sponge that you fit with care into your vaginal passageway to absorb the blood of your menstrual flow as it leaves your body. When changed regularly, this method will prevent menstruation from leaking onto your clothes. The tampon becomes saturated after some hours, depending on the time in your cycle and the heaviness or lightness of your flow. Once saturated it is time to remove and discard it. Tampons ought to be replaced every few hours, every day until your bleed is complete. Sustainable tampons made from natural sea sponge that can be cleaned and reused are available but more common, for now, are the cotton ones that come with and without applicators.

A sanitary napkin is an absorbent liner you attach to your underwear that remains there to absorb your bleed. This also needs to be changed regularly, every few hours, every day until your bleed is complete. These come in disposable cotton or can be made from a washable fabric that may be used repeatedly.

A mooncup is a small, soft, silicone cuplike vessel that you insert into your vaginal passageway to capture your menstrual flow. You only need one that you empty as needed and wash and reuse throughout your bleed. Once placed inside your vagina, you don't feel it's there.

There is also now a new wave of solutions the most popular being, absorbent underwear. You wear these undergarments instead of a tampon, sanitary napkin or mooncup (unless you feel certain days your flow is heavy enough to warrant a combined solution).

As with everything concerning your body, your choices are personal and individual. Examine your options with reverence for your body as you will be taking care of your menstrual blood for many, many years. Do so as healthfully and sustainably as feels comfortable to you.

Your body can be taken care of in simple ways, keeping it clean with bathing, but in more complex ways too: GETTING IT DIRTY IN FUN, PLAYING IN THE GRASS, THE MUD, SWIMMING IN THE OCEAN, THE LAKES, DANCING IN THE RAIN, listening to its need to feel the nature of which it is a part. *And when you bathe, allow it be a time when you refresh your body, get rid of old residue, using soaps and shampoos that are as natural as you can source, that reflect how you feel about yourself, that are gentle on your senses.* Remember, cleanliness is renewal, not a desired permanent state. To clean your body is to get it READY FOR NEW ADVENTURES ▣

YOUR BODY IS BECOMING A POWERFUL FORCE IN THE WORLD. All its potential is exploding and taking its place on the earth to become the solid basis for the expression of all you have to offer. Know this about yourself always. Be your biggest fan and your biggest supporter and when you look at yourself, admire all that you see. ADMIRE THE VERY PRIVILEGE OF BEING YOU, ALIVE TODAY, WELL AND CAPABLE OF TAKING THE TIME TO LOOK IN THE MIRROR.

ALL THESE CHANGES YOU ARE ABOUT TO EXPERIENCE ARE TRULY PROFOUND. This is a potent time that brings with it sudden shifts in perspectives, moods, and emotions, all because you are shapeshifting into a force to be reckoned with. YOU ARE BECOMING A WOMAN.

beginning

I want to tell you how you came to be. I was born, like almost all girls, with a million golden eggs inside my ovaries. Once I became a woman, every month, one or sometimes two of these golden eggs left my ovaries to embark on an adventure down a passageway inside of my body called the fallopian tube into a rich cavernous room teaming with life: my womb. In order to welcome this golden egg, my womb would add layer upon layer of thick red cushion filled with all the matter fit for sustaining life. For many, many years, each month my golden eggs found that there was nothing to meet them in this cavern that could spark them into life. Until I met your dad. He, being a boy then a man, instead of having eggs, was filled with potent, elegant wisps called sperm housed in his scrotum alongside his penis. For many, many years, his sperm would leave his body from his penis and find no eggs to marry. Then your brother came to be and rather than raising him as one, we decided to spend time together, expressing our love for each other physically. We would lie with each other and hold one another in ways that would allow our bodies to connect deeply. I would open up the gateway to my womb, through the lips of my vagina and allow him to enter me with his penis and we would let our body dance in ways that would encourage the wisps to flow out of his body and enter my womb so that on one particular day, when one of my golden eggs embarked upon its journey, there was a wisp waiting for it. And it wasn't just any golden egg nor any wisp:

IT WAS THE BEGINNING OF YOU.

That particular golden egg had an extra shimmer and the wisp had an extra sparkle and when they finally met in the cavernous place of my womb they recognized that they were always to have met. They fused together so perfectly that they became the wondrous zygote of your beginning, firmly implanting itself into the dark red cushion my womb had readied for this momentous day.

And so you started there, in that cushion. You grew and grew and grew for nine precious months until one day when you were finally ready, you decided it was time to come out. You let my body know that it was time to get ready, time to expand and contract and make way for the force of who you were to enter the world. Your head moved down my widened vagina. Special forces were released in my body that allowed me to open up to the fullest of my being to allow you out and together, we worked, pushing and giving way in the arduous beauty of birth. You arrived, sweet girl, into my arms, a beauteous wonder filled with her own golden eggs some of which may one day become children as precious to you as you are to me.

In the power of giving birth I saw the sun
in all its glory,

I saw the fear in man's eyes as he witnessed
the earthshattering strength of woman,

I saw the molten hot force that exploded
the first star,

I saw the first mover at play, I saw Life,

In a woman,

In the mightiness of her body

In the beauty of her soul

A warrior who sacrifices everything
for another.

-HOOD

1: A STATE THAT ONE FINDS ONE'S SELF IN

2: A COLLECTIVE OR COMMUNITY OF WHICH SOMETHING IS PART

being

eat

move

devote

work

rest

commune

being

Daughter you have a body, and you have a mind, and you have what many have called a soul. You are the only one who has the power to create the state you feel most comfortable in, the state of your body, the state of your mind and indeed the state of your soul. This is where you must apply your wisdom, this is where the alchemy that happens so effortlessly in your body must be mirrored by you in how you take care of your self.

YOU PLACE YOUR BEING BEFORE A MYRIAD OF ADVENTURES EVERY MINUTE AND EVERY HOUR. *And it is always your choice: you must learn that young.* You must learn that you are in charge of that to which you expose your body. You are not only what you eat, but what you do, say, hear, feel, touch. There is such strength in this and, of course the reverse, such opportunity to lose strength.

THE BEAUTY OF BEING HUMAN IS THAT WE GAIN AND LOSE STRENGTH ALL THE TIME ☑ That is how we learn, that is how we grow. When you feel depleted, take a moment, look back at what you have been experiencing in the minutes, hours, days, weeks or sometimes even years that have preceded this feeling of depletion ☑ SIT WITH YOUR THOUGHTS A MOMENT AND YOU WILL KNOW THE SOURCE OF THIS DEPLETION. ONCE YOU KNOW ITS SOURCE, IT IS FOR YOU TO DECIDE WHETHER TO CONTINUE INCLUDING IT IN YOUR LIFE OR WHETHER YOU WOULD LIKE TO FIND A WAY TO EASE IT OUT OF YOUR EXPERIENCE.

eat

EAT IN A WAY THAT YOU KNOW IS BEAUTIFUL.

Daughter, you know that good, clean fruit and vegetables should be the cornerstone of what you put into your body every day. You know that protein gives you the ability to sustain all the activity you will require of yourself, and the ability to sustain the strength required by your body. You know you need grains to satisfy hunger and give you an energy boost, and you know you need fat to help you grow. And you want food to give you pleasure and it should, but not to the extent that it is bad for you. Add sweetness to your experience, but not to the expense of your health or your mood ⚡

EAT FOOD THAT IS WORTHY
OF BEING INSIDE OF YOU. EAT
FOOD THAT HAS THE POWER
TO MATCH YOUR BEAUTY. EAT
FOOD THAT WILL INVIGORATE
YOU, INSPIRE YOU AND TREAT
YOU WITH KINDNESS AND
RESPECT.

move

MOVE IN A WAY THAT ALLOWS YOUR BODY
TO REMAIN STRONG AND SUPPLE.

The ways in which you move are infinite. The simple art of walking, walking to places instead of getting a ride, walking up stairs instead of taking an escalator or elevator, walking while hanging out with your friends instead of sitting in one spot. *Movement is an essential part of being alive*, which is why we have so many sports and physical arts to choose from to facilitate this wonderful aspect to existing.

A body that does not move sufficiently stops working to its best. Move in a way that is creative: dance, swim, run, climb trees, be silly, try yoga, or skating or fly on a trapeze. *Feel what it is to be strong.*

To have the core of what holds you up be as strong as it possibly can, bolsters all that you believe in. Allow your body be your instrument, your vessel of strength, to express what you want in the world. *Always bow to its beauty.*

THERE IS NO ONE OUTSIDE OF YOUR BEING THAT KNOWS HOW A BODY SHOULD LOOK, FOR A BODY SHOULD NOT LOOK ANY PARTICULAR WAY ⊞ There are no two bodies the same so there is no ideal. Inside of you, you know the truth of this because it sings like the wind in the trees, like an indubitable song inherent to life's rigor. How warbled it has become through the gauze of vested interests. Listen for it now, with me, listen for its potency, listen to its lyric. Go quiet inside ▢

You are beyond beautiful, you are beyond perfect, you are beyond what it is to be made of the same stuff as the stars, and the willow wisps, the lions and the mountains, the symphonies and the sun; you are beauty, inside and out ❊ TAKE HOLD OF THIS BEAUTY, LISTEN TO IT, RESPECT IT, MOVE WITH IT, BECAUSE IT LOVES TO MOVE ❊

devote

DEVOTE, TO ANYTHING.

Daughter, as you know, there are many who have gods to whom they devote in prayer, in ritual, in offerings, and many others who have ideologies to which they devote, and perhaps you do too, or will, but if you choose not to, you can devote to the tree in your backyard or the rain, or the sun, just so long as you take the time to renounce your needs and humble yourself to something you deem greater than you and to which you can be grateful.

You are so insignificant and significant at the same time and while feeling the beauty of your significance has its merits, there is also great freedom in that aspect of yourself which is insignificant, which is made insignificant by the fact that you are one minuscule part of an abundant whole. That small place of humility, when you are reminded of it, allows you the generosity to always forgive your and other's mistakes and to get up and start again with a passionate resolve that you can always be stronger as you move forward, so take the time to devote yourself to anything ✵

Arrogance is the greatest state of delusion in which one may find one's self. When you feel it coming on like the great puffed-up clown that it is, shirk it off as quickly as possible. Humble yourself to anything that comes to hand, be it as small as a raindrop: it too has ended up on this earth like you: it too will join the puddles as you do the general populous: it too will seep into the earth and pass from its time above ground, just like you. You are as big and as beautiful and as perfect as a raindrop. No more, no less. Only you get to experience it consciously. Be grateful for your smallness ▦

work

WORK IN THIS WORLD.
PRODUCE AN EXPRESSION OF YOURSELF.
BE PART OF WHAT IT IS TO BE HERE.
CONTRIBUTE. PARTICIPATE.

All this schooling, all your activities, all your youthful pass-times are there for you to discover the best use for your gifts and strengths. *They are for you to discover your noblest abilities.* WITH THIS KNOWLEDGE YOU WILL BE EQUIPPED TO CREATE HOW IT IS YOU WANT TO BE PART OF THE WORLD.

To not contribute would create a great absence in the world. To learn what it is you would like best to contribute and to do everything in your power to find a way to do it is perhaps the greatest gift you can give yourself and all of us. *Not contributing will lead to great lethargy, so let this be one of your supreme goals.* WHAT WOULD A RAINDROP BE IF IT NEVER FELL?

Let go and fall into being.

rest

REST AS THOUGH IT IS THE
GREATEST TASK OF ALL.

Nothing can come of a tired mind, body or soul. Sleeping sufficiently, and resting during the day when you feel tired will always be of the greatest benefit. Rare is the time when it is absolutely necessary for you to push beyond your body's call for rest. You must heed it. It will take its toll far beyond whatever it is you think you are missing by not listening to its call would.

But let not rest become a goal in and of itself. Laziness begets laziness. Not using the energy you have for creating expressions of yourself in the world makes it gather and stagnate inside of you, this stagnation feeling much like tiredness, or melancholy, making you feel like you have nothing to offer when in fact, the truth is simply that **YOU ARE NOT OFFERING**.

When your esteem feels low, which at times it will, make an offering of your self, sing a song, walk in the park, cook a meal, solve a math problem, come up with an experiment, invent the wheel... again, have a great conversation, listen well to a friend, do something nice for anyone, write a loving letter to someone near or far away, just be you in action and watch the melancholy lift, observe the tiredness dissipate, and all you have done is filled yourself up once again with the energy of being yourself.

commune

COMMUNE WITH THOSE AROUND YOU.
FRIENDSHIP WILL SUSTAIN YOU.
BE KIND, BE GENEROUS, CONTRIBUTE
AND ABOVE ALL ELSE, LISTEN.

There are billions of voices that want to be heard in this world. Yours is a very powerful one and it gains power from listening to the sea of other powerful voices no matter how quiet and fragile they may seem. TAKE TIME FOR YOUR FRIENDSHIPS. They are never frivolous. Sharing this world with others is one of the most important aspects of being human and, as a woman, this is doubly so. *Women generate great strength in sharing their stories with one another.* This has always been true ✖

Always be a supporter of women, in general and in the specific. Hold the best thoughts possible for your friends and even when you've been hurt by one, which you will be, or hurt another, which is most likely, take the time to go to your quiet place and forgive, yourself and the other, simply for being human, and sharing the same vulnerabilities that all young women have ever shared. Then move forward with a fresh start.

If you are shy and find that being around people is a challenge, know that it is perfectly right for you to have a smaller circle of friends throughout life. There is no need for every woman to have the hustle and bustle of large groups surrounding them. This is not for everyone. Appreciate the extra quiet that you need; there is a unique potency in this.

Whichever you are, shy or outgoing, never think that the other has it easier or harder, they are just different, both as challenging and liberating as they are made to be.

COMMUNE WITH YOUR FAMILY, THE PEOPLE
WHO BROUGHT YOU INTO THE WORLD, THE
PEOPLE THAT TUSSLE WITH YOU THE MOST,
PERHAPS KNOW YOU THE BEST, OR AT LEAST
THE LONGEST.

Respect that your family are the ones with whom you share the beginning of your life and endeavor to always remember that. *And if you feel like you are a creature from another species that was dropped into the bosom of their home and feel like they don't understand you, know that maybe they don't, but that's okay.* THEY ARE STILL THERE FOR YOU TO LEARN AND TO HOLD YOU WHILE YOU BECOME WHO YOU ARE.

And if your family hurt you, which they may, and you need to take time away from them, keep your journeying away gentle, so as not to add to the hurt.

GO SOFTLY
FROM THE
GROWLING
LION. YOUR
QUIET MAY
PROTECT
YOU MORE.

COMMUNE WITH NATURE AND ANIMALS.

This is your earth, this beautiful strong, powerful earth. Every inch of it belongs to you no matter what people and governments may say.

Respect the rules but revel in its beauty. There are oceans, forests, deserts, mountains, rivers, lakes, valleys, planes, barren and rocky landscapes, winds and rains, sun and snow, sunrises and sunsets, all there for you to uncover, discover, bathe in, revel in, play in, find strength in.

And all the other creatures that share this planet. We seem to have the upper hand as humans but, nevertheless, all animals deserve our respect. All female animals menstruate like you will, and carry their young like you might and commune with a male to make their offspring like you may also do. They share so much of our experience and feel the mightiness of the moon like us.

When you look into a deer's eyes, know that not only do you know something of her experience, but she knows something of yours.

COMMUNE WITH SPECIAL FRIENDS.

WE ARE ALL DRAWN TO CONNECT MORE
DEEPLY WITH SOME RATHER THAN OTH-
ERS. Quite young we start to begin practicing the notion
of best friends. As we get older, we realize we have many
best friends and many types of friends and among this range
we are, as young women, drawn more and more to find that
special connection to a friend with whom we start to share
more intimate moments than with others.

This intimacy starts out being emotional at first and then physical with handholding and hugs as young girls. Then, as teenagers we may start to explore what it is to kiss someone and as we get older again and become adults, our physical exploration becomes more intimate to reflect our growing responsibility in the world and our maturing ability to take care of our bodies' needs, which begin to include sexual needs.

Only as we have fully understood what it is to have agency over our bodies are we fit to make decisions as to with whom to share it.

YOUR BODY
IS SACRED
WHICH MEANS
PRECIOUS,
TO BE REVERED,
TO BE HELD UP AS
SOMETHING WITH
MEANING, VALUE,
TO BE RESPECTED,
HONORED, AND
QUITE SIMPLY,
TAKEN CARE OF.

YOUR BODY IS A VESSEL THAT CARRIES THIS PRECIOUSNESS, JUST AS A GLASS IS A VESSEL THAT CARRIES WATER, A VASE CARRIES FLOWERS, A FLUTE IS A VESSEL THAT CARRIES WIND TO MAKE MUSIC AND YOUR BODY IS A VESSEL THAT CARRIES EVERY OUNCE OF MATTER AND MAGIC THAT GOES INTO MAKING YOU WHO YOU ARE.

The ways in which you may define who you are are as plentiful as how many people there are in the world, for no two people understand the world the same way though many adhere to belief systems in the form of religions, philosophies, politics, movements.

But one thing that defines you and almost all females is your mysterious and beautiful ability to menstruate every month.

Yes, your body is sacred. It belongs to you and you alone. You may one day, when you are a mature woman, want to share it with somebody else and that day will announce itself with a great clarity inside of you and outside of you, with no pressure, no coercion and never any sense of obligation.

But that is a long way off for now. At this time, your body is yours to discover and explore and above all else to listen to, for this sacred vessel that you inhabit is full of wisdom.

DAUGHTER, you are not even holding hands yet. Perhaps only beginning to notice that there might be a special someone with whom you would like to hold hands. *Take your time with this moment, as with all moments. There is no rush. There is no race. There is no hurry.* THERE IS ONLY YOU AND YOUR BODY AND ITS HAPPINESS. LISTEN FOR ITS RHYTHM. LISTEN FOR ITS PACE. SOFTLY, SOFTLY, LISTEN TO IT NOW. *Its state. Its being.* What it is that it needs from you to make it thrive, as you lay here tonight in your bed, a girl, like many others, a young woman, amongst young women, special and powerful and true ⬛

ALCHEMY

1: POWER TO TRANSFORM SOMETHING COMMON INTO SOMETHING SPECIAL

2: medieval science and philosophy aiming to achieve the transmutation of base metals into gold, the discovery of a universal cure for disease, and the discovery of a means of indefinitely prolonging life.

beneath

wisdom

consciousness

girlness

togetherness

belief

final words

afterness

beneath

*
*
*
*
*

There is a cradle inside you. They call it a womb. This womb defines you. You are a woman. This cradle changes form. It is your chameleon. It knows how to be of comfort, how to be a map, how to shed a skin and how to begin again and again and again. It knows how to create life and how to hold it while it grows and how to let it go once it is ready to move onward and become something new.

THERE IS A GARDEN INSIDE YOU, A SECRET GARDEN THAT IS FILLED WITH WHISPERS OF GROWTH ⊠ It grows quietly every month a layer of fertile moss to soften the journey of a golden egg. The egg lingers awhile, waiting to see if there will be a companion and if one does not appear, the egg will roll out of this garden, taking with it the blanket of moss that was to have been its protector. *Together they become liquid, flowing out of you to enter the eternal sea of passing time.*

There is a throbbing inside you, sometimes that pounds against the inner cavity of the bone-walled dimension around your uterus. It is your womb at work and at play, and at rest, oscillating between the moments of its cycle, creating a torrent of blood in all its ecstatic beat, blood that will pass into the debris of life lived and a womb that is training itself to hold what is most sacred: Life.

From a young age you have learned to dance with this throbbing beat inside. You have learned to listen to its song, decipher its lyrics and listen even more carefully to its quiet pauses of reflection.

KNOW THIS BEAT.

You know your beat is right when it feels like it belongs with the skies and the stars and whispers the same tune as all that is beautiful. Never let this be disregarded. Reside, as your own particular beat's greatest protector, and champion it always.

Learn to recognize when people say your beat is wrong and find a way to hold on to your own indu-bitable knowledge that your beat is never wrong. It is essential for your survival. *It is who you are, and is forged in the most sacred hallways of creation.*

THE WORLD NEEDS YOUR SONG.

NEEDS YOUR PARTICULAR BEAUTY.
NEEDS YOUR STRENGTH

INHABIT YOURSELF
INHABIT YOUR BODY

INHABIT IT, live in it as it is yours and never disregard it.

INHABIT IT, own it as though you have understood it to be the most wonderful vessel to carry all that you have to offer, perfect in all its glory and all its quirks.

INHABIT IT, never allow another to use any part of your body for actions you do not sanction. Not your voice, nor your words, not your movement, not your body, not your touch, not your joy. You alone are the author of your being's story and the world wants to hear what you have to say.

wisdom

Wisdom is the quietest of voices that speaks under everything you witness, everything you do, everything you are.

When you are quiet, wisdom flows through you as though it is the only river you have ever known, but in the loud chaos of your day-to-day life, you may lose its soft whisper often, though know it never leaves you. There are times that even wisdom clamors to be heard and it can sound like a wild, crazy animal and though you can't help but hear it, you know it is better to find a place where you can both retreat for a while and listen to each other once again and become one so that you may speak with a gentle voice, for wisdom is gentle and graceful and belongs to you.

AND THE WISDOM THAT BELONGS TO YOU,
BELONGS TO THE WORLD.

I SAID YOU ARE FULL OF WISDOM, DAUGH-TER, AND YOU ARE. Every follicle of your being carries with it the truth. You are a sensory entity, an antennae, picking up signals from every stimulus to which you expose yourself.

You see, you hear, you smell, you taste, you touch and you feel. Your mind decodes everything into thought and your womb decodes everything into wisdom. You receive information and allow it swirl inside of you until it starts to resonate. The immaterial central column of your inner organism is the finest of tuning forks. It lets you know when you are in the presence of that which is true, that which is beautiful, that which is made up of the same stuff as the best of you, that with which you can run, play, dance, sing, be, work. It lets you know what you can breathe into your body so every millimeter of your being is filled with the makings of wisdom. It is called your intuition.

INTUITION
IS YOUR
BIRTHRIGHT.

DAUGHTER, there is a very strong chance that for you this wisdom is not so quiet. Perhaps it is the loudest response you have to everything. Perhaps that is the joy of being you. But let me tell you this: if ever you do feel like you cannot access this inner guide to truth, if you feel confused or lost, go to a quiet place or look into the sky at the bright moon and present whatever question is bothering you to that quiet. If you have trouble hearing your intuition, ask your inner wisdom to speak to you so clearly that you cannot mistake that it is your wisest voice speaking and then listen carefully; when you hear it, you will know because you will no longer feel lost, but you will feel alive and almost tingling with the truth. You may even feel it spinning in your body as you expand inside, almost as though someone inflated you like a balloon. And if you want to know if you are in the presence of something or someone or some thought that does not serve you, go quiet a moment and listen; if you feel smaller, and withered, and depleted by that thought, like that same balloon but this time without air, or worse, deflated and twisted in someone's hands. If this is the feeling, it is not wisdom. Listen until you feel full again. When you are full, you know.

All Truth which is the goal of what you seek inside of you is best accompanied by absolute humility. We are but part of a greater system, which has a driving intelligence and which shows no mercy for our whims. It is only when we listen with our most finely tuned antennae can we have a vision that will be fit to follow. If you cannot find the place of humility within your vision, your vision has no power and could slam against that of the greater wisdom to your own disadvantage.

*

*

*

*

———————————————————————

Always seek humility within. This will give you great strength and great power.

consciousness

I spoke also of consciousness, which I need to explain to you as you are but a child. The moon moves without an external guide, the cat prowls the street without an external guide. They are driven by primal forces of which they are not aware and yet, that assist them in their survival. As human beings, we are distinguished from the moon and the cat by our ability to think outside of these primal forces: we are aware of being hungry, we are aware of wanting a bed, we are aware of playing and desire and, as a result, we have the ability to choose how we approach life using this awareness as an external guide to our primal forces. But with this awareness comes the challenge of making the choices that will guide our vessels well.

Endeavor to make the most beautiful choices.

girlness

*

*

*

There is a divine strength in your flexibility. Your ability to flow like water. Your ability to change course if you feel the waters you are presented with are not fit for travel. This fluidity is nothing but a boon. Trust it. For I have seen how when girls and women try to still these waters believing they might please others, their life-force becomes stagnant and murky; clear vision is no longer possible. It is your very fluidity, Daughter, that keeps you like crystal, shimmering in elegance and light, cutting in your sharp intellect, dazzling in your radiance.

Flow alone before being stilled by a group who wish to harness your power by trapping it to use for themselves. And if you cannot escape such entrapment, find the movement inside and know that once you are free, which you will be, you will flow again without the heavy hand of order and control descending upon you, keeping your spirit down. For the only reason anyone throughout history has wanted to keep a spirit down is because they have felt unworthy of letting their own fly.

BE PROUD TO FLY

togetherness

As you journey into womanhood, so too do you journey into the giant adventure of connecting with someone deeply in affection. Use all the tools with which you were born to guide you, trusting always your inner voice, trusting always when you feel good around someone or when you don't, and if you don't, never ignore that. The more you practice this as a young woman, the stronger these reflexes will become for when you become an adult. For in adulthood, intimacy becomes more complex when you enter a world where you might choose a partner with whom to have a child and with whom to spend a large part of your life.

ALWAYS KNOW THAT YOU ARE PERFECT, AND ONLY SOMEONE WHO SEES THAT IN YOU, IS DESERVING OF YOUR AFFECTION. So for all those for whom you may seem invisible, know that your being is meant for other realms of which they are not part ☑

Love cannot be unrequited, for love is the mystical connection between two beings that see each other's beauty in all its glory.

Wait for such a love and know that it will come.

belief

All happiness is derived from what your internal state becomes. Nothing on the outside will ever change that. No material shift in your reality will ever change the spiritual state within. The reverse is not true.

If you remain constant to that voice within and listen to it with reverence and respect, your external world will reflect you in your utmost perfection. You will find everything you need and it will appear externally as you so desire. *The world is but a reflection of our inner state.*

When the world frustrates us, it is simply a way for us to know that within, we are frustrated by something about ourselves. And that we can change.

The outside is always incomplete, but it is a reflection and reflections can be important. Days are as smooth as the journeying of your heart, as rough as the terrain you may be passing over or through. In the moments that teach you struggle and difficulty, no life skates along solid ice, this reflection also serves. What is the world around you telling you today? What reflection is it holding up to you? Is there joy and bounty returning? Is there sadness and strife? What you give to the world, does it return to you? How do you mitigate the troubled times?

At night, daughter, sit down to speak, sit on the floor, so as to remember your humility before it all. Open up your hands to receive, for there is always an abundance of gifts in the quiet. Offer all of yourself to the wild and wonderful universe that shares your secrets. Pour yourself out completely into her hands. She is always waiting for you with truth, respect and kindness

As you reveal yourself each night to her, she will remind you of your magnitude and how often in your days you have made yourself small to fit into ideas of yourself that could never quite allow for such vastness ♡

THIS VASTNESS IS IN EVERYONE.

Sometimes when you embody this vastness most, you find people go silent, for what is there to say in the face of such vastness? What words could possibly match its rigor?

Those silences can embarrass you. Your greatness can embarrass you. So perhaps you shut it down. Or you trust what another says instead of trusting what you feel and every time you do that, you move further away from your essence until you are lost within your own being. But this lostness, or confusion serves you too. You know then you must spend time in your quiet place, you must spend time with your hands open, directing yourself back towards the wild and wonderful universe so you can fill up once again from her infinite well which exists inside of you and arrives once more in your being, complete to begin again.

Return your troubles in solitude and quiet. Offer them back to the vastness when no one is looking. It will take them from you, or at least ease them for a while. If you try to return them through the vessel of another, through anger, or revenge, or stress or un-kindness, you will feel a kicking, a bolting, a scream-ing coming through that vessel. For that is not the right passage for your strife.

Sit in your room and speak the words of your troubles. Deliver them into the ether through the gift of speech. Let the vessel of sound carry them out of your body to the vastness so it can change their form.

KNOW THAT THEY CAN LEAVE YOU AND THAT YOU CAN DRAW A NEW FUTURE TOWARD YOU THROUGH A NEW SET OF WORDS.

Trust in this knowing. To trust in your fears will serve only to create a nervousness in your body, an unfounded anxiety. To trust in the truth that all will be well in your world as you listen to the deepest part of your intuition and use it as your guide, will pave the way for a joyous experience of your life.

Paint the picture of the next day, how you would like it to unfold without that which troubles you.

WATCH AS YOU LEARN TO CREATE THE WORLD AROUND YOU.

This is the magic of being here. This is the magic of having faith This is the magic of being the alchemist.

A MEDITATION BEFORE INTIMACY WITH ANOTHER: Oh Great Wisdom, there is a magic inside of me! I know it intimately and long to share it with the world. You have layered me with this magic, unfolding it sheet by sheet as I have made my way thus far. It hurts when I feel it has vanished: I never want to hurt. There are people who do not believe in magic, but I know they are wrong. They have not seen inside of me. I travel within the boundaries of my being every day along the invisible pathways where everything that there is to know, is known. I have an intuition speaking to me of this knowledge, speaking to me so that I may hear, with its ears, see with its eyes, feel with its hands the everpresent beauty before me, should I wish to encounter it.

There is sadness, I have heard. There is war, which makes no sense. There are people that would like to say that if there is war there is no beauty. But I know that is not true. I know that there is only war because people have forgotten to see the field of flowers and understand that there is plenty. I know that there is hunger because someone has forgotten to share the beauty of good harvest with their neighbors. I know that there is suffering because the knowledge of beauty, and faith in love has not been passed on to all our friends. So no matter the protests of those that cite darkness, there is light and it radiates inside of me. I will do my best to share it, my utmost to see it and attempt every day to embody it fully.

Great Wisdom, inside of me, that is where it all begins, and ends, and all traveling starts out and returns. The world is vast inside of me and outside is merely a spec. To cast the inside of me in the mold of outside's expectation is to do me great harm, for I am bigger than all that any one person can see. There is no one who can see the whole of me. Only I know how big that is. Every word I speak has a root reaching deep into the bottomless well of my being. And in the very depths of that well, there is the secret of who I am and who I want to be now and always.

Who would be worthy of an invitation to see this pounding heart of my soul that carries inside of it such fragility and strength?

Who would I dare share this with knowing that whoever I show the way to, will know it forever?

Those who I let inside of me, must be worthy, for I humbly warrant great respect, great care, great reverence ▢

final words

DAUGHTER, there is a silence, unknown and known to us all which, each time we try to articulate, slips through our articulation like water in a colander. For the silence is infinite in its meaning and our words are but finite specs of metal, powerless to uphold the infinite depths of what is. But even if these words were to hold up just for a meagre moment a sense of your beauty, your power, your wisdom, your strength, they have been worth their telling. If you have caught a glimpse of the wondrousness of your existence in the moment this leaky colander has held the waters of truth, I am glad of that moment. *Let the reflection of this water shimmer in you for a lifetime.* Let no one take this knowledge away from you. Fill in the colander with your own words and experiences, so that the foundation of your being is a solid one that rests firmly in this beauty and this truth: that you are loved and revered and know how to love and revere others ▨

You are loved and revered and know how to love and revere others.

afterness

There was a Before, one would imagine, before the now of your being and one can only imagine that there is too an After. Once I have passed into that After and you are no longer walking the earth as the daughter of a flesh-laden mother, know that I will always be around you, within you, behind you, filling you still with all the love we have shared, rubbing your brow as you lay down at night, with daughters of your own and granddaughters too, sharing our truths as we are blessed to do, holding you safe from my eternal bed with all that I have thought and have in wisdom said.

ACKNOWLEDGEMENTS

With complete gratitude to my early readers, Robyn, Mariana and Duff; to all the women in my life who have taught me everything, most especially Margot, my mother, and my Betties, Louise and Karen, to Elena for inspiring me to write this as an offering to daughters everywhere, to Lauren for her devotion to this text and to the beauty of her design, to Grainne, my agent, for her constant encouragement, to my husband, Andrew, for understanding womanhood in its most alchemical way and to Willow, for whom this book came to be 🖼

Published by BlackBirch Books
An imprint of BlackBirch Incorporated
109 West 10th Street, New York, NY 10011

ISBN 978-0-9975233-0-0

1. Young Adult Health, Relationship and Personal Development
2. Girls & Women's Health
3. Young Adult Mind, body, spirit
The Alchemy of Womanhood

DESIGN BY Lauren Monchik
ARTWORK BY Su Blackwell
PHOTOGRAPH BY Yeshen Venema

Printed in the United States of America
Distributed by BlackBirch Publishing

Lovely, moving, spiritual, deep, beautiful . . .
— *Robyn Watts (Lawyer, Rights Advocate and Mother of 3)*

The words are like a poem and kept resounding in my head.
— *Karen Duffy (Writer, Actress, Television Personality, and Mother of 1)*

"The Alchemy of Womanhood" beautifully explores the wonders
of the female body . . . It is an absolutely brilliant piece of work
that I would recommend to any young girl, teenager or woman.
— *Alex (16 years old)*

Such an interesting book. It will definitely help
and inspire daughters everywhere.
— *Honey (12 years old)*

It is such a pleasure to hear a voice expressing the existence
and power of the feminine in a woman's soul, irrespective of age.
— *Tanya Minhas (Fashion designer, Artist and Mother)*

"The Alchemy of Womanhood" is unlike any development books
I read as a young teenager. And, the most unique part of the book
is that it can be shared between mother and daughter.
— *Alyssa Gustafson (Editor and Writer, 26)*

CPSIA information can be obtained at www.ICGtesting.com
Printed in the USA
LVOW11*1534220916

505790LV00013B/120/P

9 780997 523300